Tiny House Storage Ideas:

20+ Clever Storage Hacks To Use Your Small Place With Highest Effectivity

Table of content

Introduction

Small spaces have a wonderful appeal for many people these days. They're usually less expensive to rent or own than larger apartments and houses. Small living quarters are also intimate and cozy, an especially nice feature for new couples. They certainly cut down on unwanted guests. And, if you manage your storage space well, it only takes a short time each day to keep small spaces clean and tidy.

When you first see your new small space, you might wonder how you'll get everything you own inside, especially if you've been living in a larger space for a while. Although you might not be able to keep absolutely everything if you're moving from a larger home or apartment, you can use the storage ideas in this book to get the most possible storage space and keep more of your favorite possessions.

The key to organizing your small space is to look over the space you have and assess how much storage you can squeeze out of it. Before you do that, though, you need to know what kinds of spaces you can use to hold all the items you're going to keep with you and how to use them. The good news is that by the time you finish reading this book, you'll have over 20 new ideas about where and how to store your most precious and useful items!

Chapter 1 – De-Clutter Your Drawers

Drawers can be very convenient places to hide away smaller items. That is, they can be if you keep them organized. Otherwise, they can be a catch-all for things you really don't even have a use for, and they can fill up quickly until everything in them is utterly useless. After all, who has time to search through an entire drawer to find one small item? However, you can reclaim your drawers and use them to their fullest capacity. Here are some great ideas to help you do it.

1) Make Your Own Custom Kitchen Drawer Dividers

You've probably seen drawer dividers before. For instance, most people have a silverware drawer in their kitchens where they keep their knives, forks and spoons organized with a plastic divider specifically designed for that purpose. These dividers often waste space because they aren't custom-fitted to the size of your drawers. But, you can make your own drawer dividers easily with just a little planning and a few inexpensive materials.

Before you make the divider, decide what needs to go into the drawer. The items don't necessarily have to be the same types of items; they just have to be similar enough in size that they can be grouped together without losing the smaller items. Put groups of items into the drawer so that they fit together like a puzzle.

Measure the entire inside of the drawer as well as each of the sections you've made in the previous step. Measure the height of the inside of the drawer. This is the width of the board you need, Add up the measurements of all the drawer sections to get the length of the board you need. Cut the board into the lengths you measured for the sections. Put down a page of newsprint inside your drawer and lay out your drawer sections of top of it. Glue the sections together and let them dry. When the sections are thoroughly dry, remove them from the drawer and pull off the newsprint. You now have a custom-made removable drawer divider!

2) Buy Clothing Drawer Dividers

Storing clothing can be a challenge. If you don't keep your dresser drawers neat, the clothing gets into a jumbled mess. You end up choosing between ironing clothes you usually don't have to iron or wearing wrinkled clothing. Besides that, your clothing takes up more space when it isn't folded up neatly in the drawer. You can buy mesh or plastic drawer dividers to keep your clothing organized and neat.

3) Fold Clothing for Easy Access

When you fold clothing the usual way, it can be difficult to locate the garment you're trying to find. You have to lift up stacks of clothing to look underneath for the items on the bottom of the stacks. Instead, fold your clothes and stack them; then turn the stack on its side and lay it in the drawer. Once you have the idea, you can experiment with folding the clothing so it fits the drawers in this new arrangement. When you are finished, you can open your drawer and immediately see what's inside.

4) Using Hanging Baskets to Increase Your Bathroom Storage

Toiletries can take up a lot of space in your bathroom. And, in most bathrooms, there just aren't enough drawers or shelves to put them all. Here's an idea for you: Get some plastic baskets with handles and hang them from the ceiling with wide ribbons. Position them so they're easy to reach from the sink. You can use decorative baskets you buy at a craft supply store or even Easter egg baskets. Then put small, light objects in the baskets so they're right at hand when you need them.

5) Bonus: Be Creative with Small Clothing Items

Do you have a lot of scarves or other small items taking up drawers that could be used for larger clothing items? Take them out and try something new. Place a corkboard square near your dresser mirror, cover it with decorative felt, and position hooks on it. Then, you can hang up those scarves to save space and create a beautiful design at the same time.

Chapter 2 – Stow It Down Below

Walk around your small house or apartment and look for places near the floor that aren't being used in any way. You might have wasted space beneath furniture or in the bottoms of closets. You can put all that extra space to use with the following helpful tips.

6) Hide It under End Tables

If you have end tables with room underneath them, you can easily turn those wasted spaces into storage. All you have to do is to make a small tablecloth that hangs to the floor. Covering a square end table is easy. Simply measure from the floor on one side of the table, up over the table and back down to the floor. Use this measurement as one side of the tablecloth and make the other side the same length. Add 1/2 inch, cut, and sew in a hem. If you like, you can add some attractive trim around the hem as well.

If you have a round table, measure across the top to get the diameter. Then, measure from the edge of the table to the floor. Choose some inexpensive fabric that coordinates with the colors in the room where you're going to use it. Unfold the fabric and make a chalk line from the center of the fabric to the length of the diameter. From that line, use the measurement you took going to the floor and add 1/2 inch. Put a string on a pin at the center of the fabric and hold it so it reaches this point on the fabric. Move the string around the pin to mark off a circle. Cut out the circular piece of fabric, give it a quick hem and put it on top of the end table. Then, you can store anything under it that you wish.

7) Store It under the Bed

You can buy plastic storage bins designed to fit perfectly under your bed. The best kind has casters or rollers so you can easily pull it out when you need something from it.

If you don't want to spend the money on a plastic container, you can make your own from scraps you have around the house. Start with shoe boxes, shirt boxes or large flat boxes that can fit under the bed. Cover them with contact paper to make them more durable and moisture-resistant. Fill the boxes up with seasonal clothing and other items you don't use every day. Then, just slide them under the bed until you need them.

8) Use the Bottom of Your Closet
If you live in a small space, you can't afford the luxury of wasting space that could be used for storage. One place people often waste space is under their hanging clothes. Hang longer items like dresses, pants and long coats together and shorter items like shirts, blouses and shorter skirts to the other side. Underneath the shorter items, you can add a shoe rack, shoe boxes full of accessories or longer boxes containing clothing you rarely wear.

9) Stow It underneath Your Sofa
To use the space under your couch, you have to find items to store there that are fairly flat. Store board games in their original boxes. Or, you can use covered shirt boxes to store playing cards and other smaller items. To cover a shirt box, measure from one side of the box over the top and to the other side. Do the same for the shorter sides of the box. Add 1 inch to each measurement. Use each of these measurements to draw a rectangle on your fabric. Cut out a rectangle of fabric that fits over the shirt box and glue it in place using a hot glue gun. This is a great way to use this extra storage space in a decorative way to add to the appearance of the room rather than detract from it. If you're going to make a tablecloth to hide storage under your end table, you can use more of the same fabric for a color-coordinated look.

10) Use Under-Sink Organizers

The space under bathroom and kitchen sinks can become packed with a wide array of cleaning products. First, cut down on the number of products you keep. Try to choose multi-surface cleaners and floor cleaners that work on all types of floors. After you reduce the number of cleaning products you're going to store, get a plastic tote to store the remaining items. You'll be able to find what you want more easily, and you'll reduce spills under your sink at the same time.

11) Make a Pet Organizer Chest

A small dog or cat makes an ideal companion for an individual or a couple living in a small living space. But, what do you do with the pet food and all the accessories you need for your pet? You can use a toy chest or make your own pet organizer chest to store it all. The best type is one which opens up in the front and has a flat top. Store the pet food, treats, toys, leashes and other pet accessories below. Then, put the food and water dishes on top of the chest. They can stay there for a cat or you can put them down for a small dog and then store them on top between meals.

Chapter 3 – Add Shelves and More Shelves

Shelves make great storage spaces for a wide variety of clothing articles, household products, knickknacks, mementos, and yes, books. It might seem that this type of storage solution is an obvious one, but maybe it's time to rethink where you put shelves and what you put on them. Here are some interesting new ways to use shelves in your small home.

12) Frame a Doorway or Window

Short walls tend to amount to wasted space, especially if they contain a doorway or window. Try installing bookshelves to frame the door or window. Put shelves to each side to take up all the space you're not using. Add a short shelf above the doorway or window to fill in the gap between the two side shelves. Of course, you can put books on the shelf, but you can also get more creative and put items like photos, seashells, statuettes and anything else to make the look more decorative.

13) Put Linen Shelves above the Toilet

You can buy shelves that are specifically designed to be placed above a commode. These are great for storing towels, washcloths and toilet paper. If you have some scrap wood available to you, you can easily make them yourself. Take your measurements from the floor to the ceiling for the sides. For the shelf width, take a measurement across the area you have free above the toilet.

14) Enclose an Old Chimney or Air Duct

Many small homes and apartments, especially older ones, have chimneys or air ducts that are taking up space but no longer in service. You can use them as the basic structure of a set of bookshelves. Build bookshelves to fit along all exposed sides of the chimney or duct. Fill them up with your favorite books, grouping like colored spines together.

15) Add Shelves below Your TV

If you've opted for a space-saving wall mounted flat screen TV, you're already on the right track to optimizing your small space. Take it one step further by using the empty wall space under your TV for shelves to store CD's, DVD's and video games. Make the shelves as shallow as you can and still get your entertainment items inside.

16) Shelf behind Your Door

In addition to putting up shelves to frame and interior doorway, you can place shallow shelves behind your entry door. This works especially well when the door is situated near a wall. And, you can prevent the door from damaging your shelves when people throw it open carelessly. Just install a colorful rubber ball on the front of the shelf where the doorknob meets it.

17) Fill It In With Shelves

No matter how small your living quarters are, there's almost always space between furniture and walls. Fill in the space at the end or your couch or between your living room chairs with custom-fit shelves. You can have someone make them for you or get some wood, a measuring tape and some nails and do it yourself.

18) Buy plastic or wood shelves.

Place them on the upper edges of the walls next to the ceilings. These are great places to store collectibles, out-of-season decorations and other items you don't need right at hand most of the time.

19) Connect Short Walls with Shelves

Many small homes have short walls with an unused space between them. There are lots of ways you can use these areas for storage. The most efficient use of this type of space is to put shelves across between the two walls. Then, put rectangular wicker baskets on top of the shelves, filling it up to the ceiling. You can actually use just about any type of box, as long as it fits in the space and is durable enough to last through being pulled out and pushed back in over and over.

20) Put Bookshelves under Your Bed

Do you have plenty of closet space for your clothing but nowhere to put a bookshelf? Make a bookcase that fits under your bed. Be sure it has high quality rollers of casters and a heavy duty handle so you can slide it in and out. Then, just place your books inside spine-side up so you can see the titles easily.

Chapter 4 – Store It Vertically

Most people store the majority of their household items horizontally. Clothing usually goes into drawers that way, pans are usually stored bottom down in kitchen cabinets, and sheets and towels are usually stored flat in linen closets. Change directions and store as many items as possible vertically to get the most of your horizontal space.

21) Squeeze It In

To store soft items like clothing and linens vertically, you need them to be as tight in their storage place as possible. Get a box that fits the items well, and then stack them from front to back in the box. For example, you can store washcloths in a shoebox. Fold the washcloths in fourths and stack them as if you were going to lay them flat. Put one hand under them and one hand on top to turn them on their edges. Then, to keep them tightly packed in the box, push metal bookend against one end of the stack. Or, you can use any solid item to take up the extra space. Remember to keep tightening the stack as you use from it.

22) Use a Vertical File

Paperwork is often stored vertically. You can also use a vertical file to store other flat items around your home. Get a box and some hanging folders to go in it. Then, hang anything that will fit inside the folders. In addition to warrantees, greeting cards, recipes and other paperwork, you can also put sheets and pillowcases, cloth diapers or anything you can fold up neatly into other file folders.

23) Put Vertical Dividers in a Cabinet

Pans in cabinets can quickly become disorganized. Besides that, it can be hard to get out one item in the stack without toppling the whole mess. And, at the top of the stack of pans, there is usually wasted space because the pans won't stack that high. Add vertical dividers to one of your cabinets so you can store cookie sheets, baking pans, muffin pans, skillets, pan lids and cookbooks on end, using all the available space and keeping things tidy at the same time.

24) Make Your Jewelry into Wall Art

Get any type of bulletin board. If you don't like the looks of it, cover it in an attractive fabric and staple the fabric to the back. Then, you can stick pushpins into it and hang jewelry there in a pleasing design. For a festive room, use colorful pushpins and for a more sophisticated look, you can use black, white or clear pushpins.

25) Use an Old Library Trick for Hanging Newspapers and Magazines

Although libraries are slowly phasing out paper books and periodicals, many still keep the most popular ones at hand. To save space and make them easy to find, they hang them on dowel rods. Make a frame for the rods using narrow boards, attach the rods to the boards with wood glue, let them dry and attach them to a wall near your favorite reading chair or bed. Drape the magazines and newspapers, each over its own dowel rod.

26) Make an Ironing Board Cabinet

Make a cabinet with an interior just deep enough, tall enough and about 10 inches wider than you need to store your ironing board. Put two boards, one on each side of the back so they're positioned right to hang your ironing board. Then, put a small shelf on each side to hold your iron and spray starch.

Chapter 5 – Hang It

Hanging items take up less space, and the space they do take up is usually not used for anything else. Here are some unique ways to use the space overhead in your small living quarters.

27) Hook It
Buy some heavy duty plant hooks and screw them into your ceiling. You can hang your bicycle from the ceiling so it doesn't take up any floor space. Use your imagination to think of other items you can hang from the hooks. And, you can always hang your plants there if nothing else.

28) Velcro It
Velcro is one of the handiest products for storage in small spaces. You can mount self-adhesive Velcro onto a finished board and place it on a wall or the back of a door. Then, place pieces of the other side of the Velcro on items you want to attach to it. For larger items, use commercial grade Velcro. Items can hang vertically from the Velcro holder, leaving little to no intrusion into your room.

29) Clothespin It
Clothespin scarves, ties, belts and other long clothing items to a hanger in your closet. If you have a lot of pantyhose and tights filling up an entire dresser drawer, make a hanger for them and hang in your closet. To make it, sew two large handkerchiefs together, leaving one end open to take items out and put them in. Clothespin one side of the open end to a clothing hanger.

30) Make a Hanging Kitchen Display

Would you like to have the kitchen of a professional chef? You might not be able to get large stainless steel appliances or double ovens, but what you can do is have a hanging display of kitchen items you use often. Hang up cooking pots and pans and utensils overhead above a kitchen island or over the counters. Everything is easy to reach when you need it, and your display adds an interesting touch to your kitchen.

31) Make a Compact Entry Space with a Place to Hang Coats

If your small space doesn't have a large entryway or coat closet, you can create a small entry area complete with a seat and hangers for coats. Start by building a bench with storage below. It can be as long as you have space for in your entry area. Put cushions on the bench so it can be used as spare seating and as a place to sit while taking off boots and shoes. Then, put hooks above the bench for hanging coats. Alternatively, you can make a simple coat rack with a finished board the length of the bench. Screw on large, old doorknobs to use as coat hangers and mount the board above the bench.

32) Use Hooks to Hang Utensils

Key hangers are great for hanging your car keys and house keys. Do you know what else they're good for? You can also put one by your back door and hang grilling tools there. Use cup hooks to hang your colander and strainers above the sink. A hook beside your stove can hold spoons, spatulas and whisks you use while cooking.

33) Make a Hanging Pocket Rack for Odds and Ends

To make a hanging pocket rack, cut rectangular pieces of fabric 8x10 inches. Hem up each side of each piece and sew it to a large piece of fabric. Fold over the top of the large piece and sew it down to make a rod pocket. Use a curtain rod to hang this handy pocket rack. You can put various odds and ends inside the pockets, such as scissors, tape, tapered candles, shoe horns, and just about anything you can think of that you don't have anywhere else to stow. If you don't feel like making this, you can buy a premade cloth shoe rack and use its pockets the same way. By the way, you can also use a cloth shoe organizer velcroed or stapled to the inside of a cabinet to store cell phones, their cords and other electronic devices.

34) Net It
Make a vertical net holder for shower poufs, bars of soap, nail brushes, bath mitts and other items you use in the shower or bathroom. Start with a piece of net fabric about a foot longer than the distance from ceiling to floor. Tie knots ever few feet to make individual holders. Then, gather up one end and secure it to the ceiling beside or in the shower. Place your items resting on each knot.

35) Hang It Up On Clipboards
Are you wondering what to do with your mail now that you no longer have room for an entry table? Make a wall of hanging clipboards. You can cover and design them any way to coordinate with your walls. Then, hang mail, tickets, receipts and other paper items you need to keep at hand right on the clipboard the same way you usually clip notebook paper to them.

36) Hang It Out to Dry
You can hang towels to dry in your small home even if you don't have enough towel bar space. Make a loop with a piece of twill fabric and sew the ends together, one loop on the corner of each towel. Place medium-sized hooks on your wall above your bathroom or kitchen window. It's a great way to store wet bath towels, hand towels, washcloths and kitchen towels.

37) Hang More

You can use heavy duty hooks to hang TV trays on the wall rather than storing them in a bulky TV tray stand. Placed individually side by side, they take up almost no room at all. You can use the same method to hang folding chairs to keep them neatly on hand for the next time friends drop by your small home.

Chapter 6 – Build It In

If you own your small home or apartment, or are allowed to modify it, you can get even more storage space by building it into the existing structure. You don't need elaborate building plans or fancy equipment. All you need are the basics: a measuring tape, a hammer or screwdriver, nails or screws, and a bit of paint.

38) Build in a Recessed Cabinet behind the Bathroom Door

Do you have a wall behind your bathroom door? If so, it's the perfect place for a hygiene products cabinet. Get a stud-finder to find two studs to put the cabinet between inside the wall. The standard distance from stud to stud is 15 and 1/2 inches. Use a jigsaw to cut a hole between the studs. Make your cabinet to fit the hole, and about 4 inches deep. Add a cabinet door, which you can buy premade for a 16-inch cabinet or build it yourself.

39) Build Storage under the Staircase

If your staircase has one or both open sides, you can fit lots of storage underneath it. Make several vertical dividers from large sheets of plywood and connect them to the bottom of the staircase as well as the side if one side is closed. Then, you can add shelves across some of the resulting spaces. Add clothing rods in other spaces to use for hanging items.

40) Build Storage on a Wide Staircase

You can also build in storage on top of a staircase. Start with the bottom step. Build a storage case or bookshelf with one end matching to the front of the bottom step. Then, add another storage case with one end matching to the front of the second step. Keep building upwards until you reach the top step. You can make the cases as deep as you like, as long as you keep enough room to go up and down the stairs.

41) Use the Corners

Talk about wasted space! Corners are rarely used in most homes. Build in corner bookshelves, knickknack displays of china cabinets. Use up all the corners in your small space and you'll instantly have much more storage than you ever had before.

42) Put Your Dresser in the Wall

Is your bedroom too small to keep a dresser in it? If it is, you can still have dresser space by building it into the wall. Get a new or gently used square chest of drawers. Make a hole for it in the wall and slide it in. Make sure to finish the edges of the wall beside your slide-in dresser so it looks like it was built in when the home was constructed.

43) Make a Recessed Window into a Reading Space

If you have any large recessed windows, they're the ideal place to put custom built bookcases. Build shelves across the top of the window and down along each side. Then, add a bench along the bottom with plenty of soft pillows for a cozy reading nook.

44) Make a Closet Laundry Room

Do you have a large closet you can spare but no laundry room? You can turn the closet into a handy space for your washer, dryer and all the cleaning products you could ever want. You need to run water to the closet and install a vent for the dryer, so a little expert help is nice to have. You can add shelves on the back of the closet door – either bought from a store or made with your own hands.

45) Make Slide-Out Shelves beside Appliances

If you have a space between your refrigerator and the wall, you can put slide-out shelves there. Even if the space is only a few inches wide, it's wide enough to store a single row of standard canned goods for the full height and depth of your refrigerator. This project requires precision, so it's best to ask someone experienced in woodworking or cabinetmaking to do the job for you.

46) Build Your Own Sleeping Loft

Do you have to choose between a bed and storage space? If your bed doesn't have anywhere to store anything beneath it, maybe you should get a different kind of bed. One option is to build a large, heavy duty storage case with the top dimensions the size of your mattress. You need a ladder to climb up to your sleeping loft as well. Inside the case, you can install shelves, clothing rods and/or hooks to get the most out of the space below the bed.

Conclusion

Are you ready to get the most storage space possible out of every square inch of your small house or apartment? Assess your home, looking for any unused space. Use the ideas in this book as a starting point to fill in those spaces with personal items, grooming tools, clothing, linens, books and any other items you don't want to sell or give away. Adapt the ideas to fit your unique situation, items to store and spaces to fill.

If you're brave enough, you can use the ideas in this book as inspiration for your own storage ideas. It just takes creativity and a little work to transform your useless space into storage space for your most precious personal treasures. Begin the process today and soon you will have everything you need right at your fingertips and your small home will look less cluttered than it ever has before.

Made in the USA
Middletown, DE
15 October 2023